Walther Ziegler

Heidegger
in 60 Minutes

Translated by
Alexander Reynolds

My thanks go to Rudolf Aichner for his tireless critical editing; Silke Ruthenberg for the fine graphics; Lydia Pointvogl, Eva Amberger, Christiane Hüttner, and Dr. Martin Engler for their excellent work as manuscript readers and sub-editors; Prof. Guntram Knapp, who first inspired me with enthusiasm for philosophy; and Angela Schumitz, who handled in the most professional manner, as chief editorial reader, the production of both the German and the English editions of this series of books.

My special thanks go to my translator

Dr Alexander Reynolds.

Himself a philosopher, he not only translated the original German text into English with great care and precision but also, in passages where this was required in order to ensure clear understanding, supplemented this text with certain formulations adapted specifically to the needs of English-language readers.

Dasein always understands itself in terms of its existence – in terms of a possibility of itself: to be itself or not itself.[1]

Bibliographic Information held by the German National Library: The details of the original German edition of this publication are held by the German National Library as part of the German National Bibliography; detailed bibliographical data can be found online at www.dnb.de.

© 2016 Dr Walther Ziegler
1st Edition June 2016
Jacket design and graphic design for the whole book: Silke Ruthenberg, making use of illustrations by:
Raphael Bräsecke, Creactive – Studio for Advertising, Comics & Illustrations
© JackF - Fotolia.com (image-frames)
© Valerie Potapova - Fotolia.com (image-frames)
© Svetlana Gryankina - Fotolia.com (speech-balloons)

Publisher and Printing:
BoD – Books on Demand, Norderstedt
ISBN 9783741227752

Inhalt

Heidegger's Great Discovery	7
Heidegger's Central Idea	17
Man's "Being-In-The-World"	17
Dasein's Basic Character of "Care"	22
Dasein as "Being-Toward-Death"	27
The Flight into the "They"	32
Anxiety in the Face of Nothingness	36
The Call of Conscience	42
Authentic and Inauthentic Existence	48
Becoming Guilty Vis-à-Vis One's Own Existence	52
Man in the "Enframing" of Technology, and the "Turning"	58
Of What Use is Heidegger's Discovery for Us Today?	69
Openness to the Mystery in the Age of Technology	69
Anxiety is Part of Life – Existence as Potentiality	75
Breaking Away from the Anonymous "They"	79
Living with Mortality – Living with Resoluteness!	86
Bibliographical References:	93

Heidegger's Great Discovery

Whoever takes an interest in philosophy is sooner or later bound to encounter the 'philosophy of being' of Martin Heidegger (1889-1976). His writings are worth reading, whether one opts, once one has read them, to damn him, critique him, or celebrate him as one of the 20th Century's most brilliant thinkers. There are few thinkers, indeed, about whom opinions diverge so widely. But whatever personal judgment the reader may finally form, he will always have been enriched by engagement with Heidegger's ideas.

It was in 1927 that Heidegger published the 400-page work that made his name: *Being and Time*. Despite the strange new language in which it was written – or perhaps because of it – it became a worldwide best-seller. Heidegger is still today, with Sartre, one of the key representatives of existentialism. He called his philosophy "fundamental ontology" because it was his aim to reveal the deepest foundations of how people understand the world.

Zoology, for example, cannot count as a fundamental ontology but only as an individual one: namely, as the logic or the doctrine of animals. Geology, likewise, is specifically the logic of the earth; biology the logic of *bios* (i.e. living things); sociology the logic of society etc. Each of these sciences investigates the logic of just one *part* of the realm of being. This is why they are individual ontologies: doctrines of just sections of being as a whole. They talk, respectively, of how animals, the earth, the biocosmos, and society are constituted and of the laws each obey. But Heidegger's point is that all these individual ontologies proceed, in their respective inquiries into truth, from something more fundamental which has, itself, never been inquired into: namely, the very capacity of Man to inquire into and understand things. Heidegger thus analyses in his "fundamental ontology" the basic form of Man's existence as a meaning-comprehending being who is in the world and perceives it. His interest goes beyond the individual sciences to what underlies them: the meaning of life as a whole. His main question thus runs: "what is the meaning of being?"

But if we are to ask about the meaning of being and thus of life, argues Heidegger, we must first inquire into the nature of the entity that poses this strange question. This entity is Man himself, or (to use the term by which the (self-)questioning human individual is still denoted even in English translations of *Being and Time*) human *Dasein*:

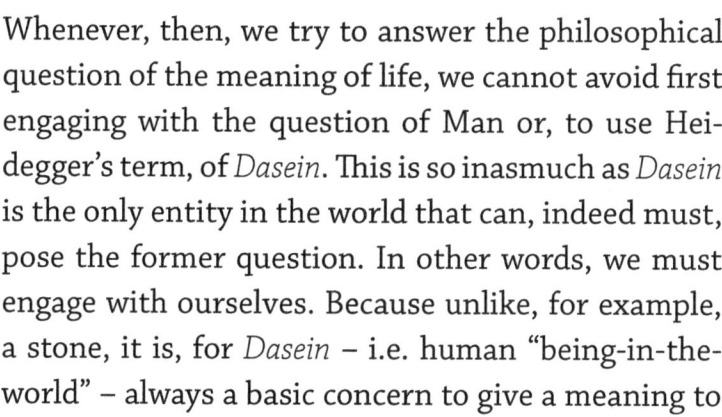

> Thus to work out the question of being adequately we must make an entity – the inquirer – transparent in his own being [...]. This entity, which each of us is himself and which includes inquiring as one of the possibilities of its being, we shall denote by the term *Dasein*.[2]

Whenever, then, we try to answer the philosophical question of the meaning of life, we cannot avoid first engaging with the question of Man or, to use Heidegger's term, of *Dasein*. This is so inasmuch as *Dasein* is the only entity in the world that can, indeed must, pose the former question. In other words, we must engage with ourselves. Because unlike, for example, a stone, it is, for *Dasein* – i.e. human "being-in-the-world" – always a basic concern to give a meaning to this being. Heidegger formulates this as follows:

> *Dasein* is an entity [...] distinguished by the fact that, in its very being, that being is an issue for it.³

The term "entity" (literally, "thing that is") is a rather technical philosophical term that needs clarification. When Heidegger says that *"Dasein* is an entity" he means that an existing human being is, with his feet, arms, legs, belly and head, a physical thing present in the world just like a stone is present in it. In this sense, stone and human being are both entities, "things that are". But whereas the stone is only a "thing that is", the human being is something more: namely, a "thing that is" for which this "is" is – as Heidegger puts it – "an issue". Unlike the stone, the human being is concerned by his own life. One might, then, restate Heidegger's claim: *"Dasein* is an entity distinguished by the fact that, in its very being, that being is an issue for it" in clearer language as: "Man is a living being for whom the life that he is living is a matter of basic concern."

Heidegger's starting point, then, is clear. To answer the great question as to the "meaning of being", he first examines that understanding of what it is "to be" which is implicit in the everyday life of human beings.

It is precisely from the "everyday", Heidegger argues, that one learns a lot about the structure and functioning of human life:

Everydayness does not coincide with primitiveness, but is rather a mode of *Dasein*'s Being, even when that *Dasein* is active in a highly developed and differentiated culture – and precisely then.[4]

Moreover, human beings succeed, in everyday life, in giving meaning to things around them and to themselves each time they say or think that something "is". That is to say, we human beings all have an implicit understanding of being and move through the world as "understanders".

We say, for example, each day such things as "the bus is late", "the weather is cold", "my heart is not in it" or "the world is not fair". This word "is" may appear, at first sight, to be completely harmless and unimportant. But Heidegger takes it as the starting point for a profound analysis of the whole of human life. Our everyday use of such terms as "is" and "be" reveals, argues Heidegger, something very special: namely, the fact that we are constantly interpreting the world in one way or another:

> Whenever one cognizes anything or makes an assertion, whenever one comports oneself toward entities [...] some use is made of 'being', and this expression is held to be intelligible 'without further ado', just as everyone understands 'the sky *is* blue', 'I *am* merry', and the like. But [...] this average kind of intelligibility [...] makes manifest that [...] we already live in an understanding of being and that the meaning of being is still veiled in darkness.[5]

What is Heidegger telling us here? He is telling us that, on the one hand, each time we say "is", even if it is only in such seemingly banal phrases as "the sky is blue", "I am merry", or "the universe is endless", we ascribe "without further ado" a meaning or a sense to the things around us (blueness to the sky, merriness to oneself, endlessness to the universe and so on). But on the other hand, he adds, the meaning of life as a whole – or "the meaning of being" – remains at the same time "veiled in darkness".

This means that the "everyday understanding of being" that humans possess is only a first indication or clue, a mere point of departure for the answering of the question of being's meaning. But what does this initial human "understanding of being" consist in? Does each human person have his own? Do we each interpret our world in our own way? How do we order the world(s) that we interpret? And above all: can we succeed, through these everyday individual world-interpretations, in understanding the meaning of being as a whole?

It was just this that Heidegger tried to do. His "phenomenological" analysis consisted in investigating *Dasein*, step by step, on the basis of just these "self-relations" that form our everyday experience. He reveals here a whole set of what he calls *existentialia*

– another coinage of Heidegger's own by which he means: ways of being that are directly and essentially typical of human beings, that characterize human life *per se*, and that cannot be shaken off by anyone humanly alive in the world. Are there really such things? Do all living human beings really share one set or structure of "ways of being"?

Heidegger's answer is a clear "yes". His phenomenological deduction of these *existentialia* in which all our lives are played out is as exciting as a whodunit. Starting from the discovery that a human being is "always already" understanding the world around him, interpreting it, and thus making himself a place in it, Heidegger names *Dasein*'s first essential state or structure "being-in-the-world".

But this 'being-in-the-world" he sees as characterized in its turn by an encompassing structure of care: namely, care about one's own life. We "care", indeed, every day in the sense of worrying about our food, the money we need to live, our health, our friends, children and family. But when he speaks of "care" as a basic existential state of human *Dasein*, Heidegger does not mean these many individual worries but rather a structural condition of "concernedness" that follows necessarily from *Dasein*'s knowing that it is defencelessly exposed to the past, present and future world. And this structural "concernedness" compels us to make, again and again, decisions relative to all of these.

The fact that we must constantly choose one possibility and thereby necessarily forgo others entails the risk that we may choose wrongly. Heidegger proposes the provocative thesis that most people do indeed choose wrongly, missing the true meaning of their lives and living out an "inauthentic" existence.

He confronts us here with the fact that we usually do only that which is modern and what "one" is supposed to do in every situation. "One" goes to school and then to university and then to work; "one" earns as much money as possible; "one" goes on holiday; "one" keeps fit; "one" puts off what can't be done now to another day. This "one", however, is not our own authentic self. Instead of bringing our own life to realization, we follow paths already trodden out by others.

Heidegger also confronts us with the reality of our own death, something that we would gladly ignore. But he also gives concrete indications of how we can make this fearful reality play a positive role in our lives. He points up, for example, the forces of self-healing contained in human *Dasein* even when it has lost its sense of security in being and faces nothingness.

This analytic of "being-in-the-world" developed by Heidegger is now almost a century old but has lost nothing of its enormous attraction. The existential structures of human *Dasein* as Heidegger revealed them remain both valid and fascinating. Hardly any reader of *Being and Time*, even today, will fail to recognize something of himself and of his own life-experiences in these structures. The language in which the book is composed strikes us still, indeed, with its many novel coinages and compound words like "being-in-the-world", as a strange one. But it is the power of this strangeness along with the force of the ideas themselves that draws readers deeper and deeper into the maelstrom of Heidegger's existential analysis.

Heidegger's Central Idea

Man's "Being-In-The-World"

Heidegger applied a method of philosophical inquiry, quite new in his day, called "phenomenology". One must not, argued Heidegger, follow modern science in slipping a ready-made catalogue of questions over the object one is inquiring into, because then the only answers one will get back will be those already contained in the question. The good philosopher simply exposes himself, disinterestedly and without pre-judgment, to the effects exerted on him by phenomena. Or, as Heidegger puts it, phenomenology means:

> Let that which shows itself be seen from itself in the very way in which it shows itself from itself.[6]

Heidegger used this phenomonological method, taken over from his teacher Husserl, to arrive at a radically new perspective on Man and the world. Earlier philosophers, like Descartes or Kant, had always assumed these two things to be separate entities. But Heidegger claims that, phenomenologically considered, Man and the world are one thing. Our perception of ourselves, he argues, is inseparably bound up with our perception of the world; as soon as we open our eyes we already find ourselves locked into a stream of impressions and sensations. So it is not as if I am first there existing as "I myself", an abstract subject, and only then hear the alarm-clock ring and look to see what time it is; rather, both these things – the perceiving "I" and what it perceives – come into being in the same moment. As soon as I direct my attention to a thing, I am myself in the midst of this thing. Because, as Heidegger writes,

> When Dasein directs itself toward something and grasps it, it does not somehow first get out of an inner sphere in which it has been proximally

> encapsulated, but its primary kind of being is such that it is always 'outside' alongside entities which it encounters and which belong to a world already discovered.[7]

Thus, Heidegger speaks no longer of Man, as subject, on the one hand and the world, as object, on the other but rather of "being-in-the-world". This is his attempt to overcome the subject-object division that had dominated philosophy before him and that he believed to be artificial and false.

He also emphasizes that *Dasein*, as "being-in-the-world" is not only an entity that is always rationally interpreting the world but also one that is always emotionally affected by it. We are at every moment subject to one or another sort of "mood". This was a fact entirely overlooked by Kant and rationalistic philosophy. We may be happily excited, or bored, or keyed up, or jolly, or depressed. But we are always in some sort of "mood", even if this is just a mood of emptiness or dullness. Through our moods our being-in-the-world is disclosed to us in a way that precedes all rational knowledge:

> The fact that moods can deteriorate and change over means simply that in every case Dasein always has some mood [...]. A mood makes manifest 'how one is and how one is faring'. In this 'how one is', having a mood brings Being to its 'there'.[8]

The way we perceive the world depends, then, on our mood. The same object can be perceived very differently depending on the mood of the perceiver. An oak tree will not be perceived in the same way by the fox hiding in terror among its roots from the hunter as it will be by the woodpecker building his nest in its branches; or by the squirrel springing happily from branch to branch; or by the courting couple kissing underneath its boughs; or by the woodsman who has laboriously to chop it down.

To a person in a low mood everything may "look grey".

His depressed "being-in-the-world" makes him perceive the whole world, along with his "being-in-it", as dark and gloomy. Likewise, a man in a happy mood sees everything "through rose-tinted glasses".

The "how one is" of "being-in-the-world", then – which discloses to *Dasein* the world it inhabits and its own self – is an inescapable part of what it is to be human. It is a basic "mode of (human) being" of the class of Heidegger's *existentialia* – as is the second such mode of *Dasein* that he calls "care".

Dasein's Basic Character of "Care"

Here we come to a further key phenomenological finding of Heidegger's regarding the structure of human life. *Dasein*, says Heidegger, is not just an entity which, like a stone, is simply "there"; rather, it is always "a step ahead of itself":

In each case Dasein is already 'ahead of itself' in its being.[9]

What does Heidegger mean by this? He describes here a "how we are" that is structurally common to all human *Dasein*: namely, that we are constantly concerned about the world, our fellow men, and of course our own selves. Our *Dasein* can never be contained just in the present moment. Man lives not just in the "now". He is always forming projects and thus projecting his own being into the future. Man is always "ahead of himself" because the "vision" that guides his life is always a *"pro-vision"*. He makes *"pro-vision"* for the next moment, the next day, the next week, or his old age. He *"pro-vides"* for the family evening meal and for his children, so that every present moment involves a "care" not only for what is but also for what was and will be. Our "being-in-the-world" is thus always a *caring* being, always related and referred to what awaits us and approaches us from out of our world. Our being, says Heidegger, is always a "being-out-toward-something":

> In the directed, caring 'being-out-toward-something', the 'that-with-respect-to-which' of life's care, the world, at any given time, is there, present.[10]

But by stating this character of "care" to be one of the basic *existentialia* of *Dasein*, or life as a human being, Heidegger means more than just our individual daily cares and more than just the plans and projects we form for the future. He refers here rather to the even more basic fact that, as beings existing in space and time, we must not only form projects but must constantly "pro-ject" ourselves, in our very being, out of ourselves into the world. (The German word Heidegger uses here, *Entwurf*, drew German readers' attention to the concrete meaning of this term "project" in a way that the Latin-based English word does not. A "project" is, concretely. a "throwing forward"; to "project oneself" is thus, concretely, to be "thrown" into the world.) Heidegger stresses the "must" here. A human being cannot decide simply to stop caring about past, present and future and cease, for example, to form future-related projects. Because to make no more plans or projects for the future and to simply sit quietly in a corner is still, in the sense that Heidegger gives to the term, a project. This passivity too is a way of "throwing oneself into being" and becoming a particular kind of person: in this case, a passive person who sits quietly in a corner with no plans. There is no escaping, then, from the "projective" character of *Dasein*:

Dasein [...] as long as it is [...] is projecting.[11]

Heidegger's Central Idea

Equally inescapable, then, is *Dasein*'s character of "care". "Care" belongs to the basic *existentialia* of human life because there is no way of getting around this having to "project ourselves" into one or another possible present or future way of being. It is in the passages where he deals with this theme that Heidegger's insistence on drawing abstract terms like "projection" back to their original, concrete meaning is most clearly displayed. He describes *Dasein* not just as necessarily "(self-)projecting" but as "thrown" into existence. Since no one asks us, before our birth, whether we want to live "projectively" in the world or not, our existence is itself a "thrown-ness". We must make the best of what we are "thrown into", regardless of where, when, or in what condition we are born. And this is not without consequences. Because, since *Dasein* is constantly "pro-jecting" ("throwing") itself into a possible future, it is in a constant process of restructuration:

> Because of the kind of being which is constituted by the 'existentiale' of pro-jection, *Dasein* is constantly 'more' than it factually is [...].[12]

We are "constantly more than we factually are", says Heidegger, because our (self-)pro-jection toward the future always has an effect also on our present. A leading athlete, for example, derives from the idea alone that he might win a medal at the next Olympics a powerful motivation to train hard in the present. An athlete "pro-jecting" himself as a future victor, then, is already more than just an athlete in training. He is already a potential victor, a "winner", even if the race has not yet been run. As Heidegger puts it:

As 'being-possible' [...] Dasein is [...] that which it is *not yet*.[13]

It is this structural possibility of "pro-jecting" oneself as something more, or other, than one is that constitutes the "care" character of *Dasein*. We can "pro-ject" ourselves anew at any moment, by moving from the country to the city, starting a family, gaining new friends, changing our job, or even "dropping out" entirely and becoming a Trappist monk.

But at this point there arises, at the horizon of the "care" character of *Dasein*, a new and important question. Are my possibilities really unlimited? Does death, in the end, not cut off all my opportunities? How much time do I really have for these self-projections and self-developments?

Dasein as "Being-Toward-Death"

Some people, perhaps, would gladly live forever, but the fact is we all must die. We are not asked before birth whether we want to be mortal or immortal but are, as Heidegger says, "thrown" into life: a life already fixed as having to end in death.

> *Dasein*, as thrown 'being-in-the-world', has in every case already been delivered over to its death. In being towards its death, *Dasein* is dying factically and indeed constantly [...].[14]

That we all must "factically" (i.e. really) die at some point is easy enough to understand. But in what sense are we dying "constantly"? By using this word Heidegger wants to make it clear to us that we draw, with every day, hour and second, inexorably a little nearer to death. He expresses this brutally but precisely when he writes:

The 'end' of 'being-in-the-world' is death.[15]

This is why, for Heidegger, every *Dasein* is a 'being-toward-death'. But with this phrase he stresses not just the fact that we are all mortal but also that we all must deal with this in some way. We must come to terms with death and adopt an appropriate stance toward it. We basically have two possible ways of dealing with lives that we know must end in death, or with our "being-toward-death", as Heidegger puts it. We can either suppress this certainty of death or let it remain part of our awareness. Generally, people prefer to suppress it, since the idea of death is hard to bear. To suppress this idea is not, of course, to believe one will never die, which is impossible for a rational being. It is to push death into some indefinite future. As Heidegger writes:

> One says: 'death certainly comes, but not right away'. With this 'but...' the 'they' denies that death is certain. [...] Death is deferred to 'some time later' and this is done by invoking the so-called 'general opinion'.[16]

"General opinion" does indeed hold that average life expectancy in Europe will soon attain ninety years, so it is easy for the common 'they' to shelve all thought of death:

> The 'they' does not permit us the courage for anxiety in the face of death.[17]

Heidegger urges us, however, not to retreat from this certainty of death but to consciously "anticipate" the fact of our own eventual demise. Once we have clearly grasped the fact that we will die, this certainty will compel us to see our own life in the limitedness of its possibilities. And precisely this can help us to live more resolutely, i.e. in accordance with our own, instead of with the "general", opinion:

> The entity which anticipates (its own death) [...] is forced by that very anticipation into the possibility of taking over from itself its inmost being, and doing so of its own accord.[18]

What does Heidegger mean here when he speaks of the anticipation of death's "forcing us to take over from ourselves our inmost being, and to do so of our own accord"? Do we not do this anyway? Does each of us not live his own life? And does he not do so "of his own accord", forming his life in terms of his own personal wishes and goals?

Heidegger denies that this is so. He makes the provocative claim that in daily life we are generally not "ourselves" and let ourselves, without noticing it, be guided by interests other than our own:

Perhaps when Dasein addresses itself in the way which is closest to itself, it always says 'I am this entity' and in the long run says this loudest when it is '*not*' this entity.[19]

In Heidegger's phenomenological analysis the answer to the question "who is *Dasein*?" is often not, if we consider just the everyday and the average, "us ourselves" but rather "they, the others". For this reason Heidegger calls this astonishing shift of self-responsibility *Dasein's* "falling under the sway of the 'they'".

The Flight into the "They"

If we allow ourselves to "fall" in this way, we no longer do what we want to do but only what we see "those around us" do:

We take pleasure and enjoy ourselves as *they* take pleasure; we read, see and judge about literature and art as *they* see and judge; likewise we shrink back from the great mass as *they* shrink back; we find 'shocking' what *they* find shocking.[20]

This way of life is very comfortable and thus very widely adopted. But in the end it is a flight from reality. Because the "care" character of *Dasein* demands that, where *Dasein* is authentic, it is we ourselves who experience this "care" and we ourselves who choose our life-projects. Where *Dasein* slips into the inauthentic mode of a "falling under the sway of the 'they'", the form given to *Dasein*'s caring "being-in-the-world" becomes a matter left up to others. One orients one's life solely by what "most people think", that is, by general rules and conventions that represent both everybody and nobody:

> So *Dasein* makes no choices, gets carried along by the 'nobody', and thus ensnares itself in inauthenticity. This process can be reversed only if *Dasein* specifically brings itself back to itself from its lostness in the "they".[21]

But how can this be done? How can *Dasein* "bring itself back" to itself again? Heidegger's answer is logically consistent. Where a human *Dasein* has, for a long time, mostly been shirking taking its own decisions – having opted, at some point, to lead a life in which others make decisions for it – *Dasein* needs to reverse this flight into the "they" and make another choice. *Dasein* must choose to once again decide for itself:

> When Dasein thus brings itself back from the "they", the "they-self" is modified in an existentiell manner so that it becomes *authentic* "being-one's-self". This must be accomplished by *making up for not choosing*.[22]

"Making up for not choosing" means that we decide to no longer let ourselves be manipulated and to choose and seize, in future, our own life-possibilities. For this reason Heidegger speaks of "choosing to make a choice":

> In choosing to make this choice, Dasein makes *possible*, first and foremost, its authentic potentiality-for-being.[23]

But this, says Heidegger, is no easy matter. Someone who has let their existence be guided, for months, years or even all their life, by the anonymous "they" cannot simply say: "starting tomorrow I will decide for myself". The "they-self" is very firmly rooted in many of us and an existential crisis, in which the "they"-world collapses, is usually required in order to free us and give us the sense of being able once again to grasp our potential for being ourselves.

But such crises, says Heidegger, go essentially hand in hand with a mood which pervades and takes hold of our existence as a whole. It is an uncanny mood which isolates us, throws us back on ourselves, and puts all our past life into question. He calls it *anxiety* (although the mood referred to has also been called, in existentialist literature, "dread"). Anxiety menaces and shakes us in our deepest foundations and yet, argues Heidegger, it also opens up for us a chance to find our true selves.

Anxiety in the Face of Nothingness

Heidegger speaks of anxiety as a "basic state of mind" and makes an essential distinction between it and the everyday phenomenon of fear. Fear is distinguished by the fact that one fears something specific. It always has a concrete object. One fears, for example, being bitten by a dog, being struck by lightning in a storm, or being robbed. But the state of mind of anxiety is something uncannily non-specific:

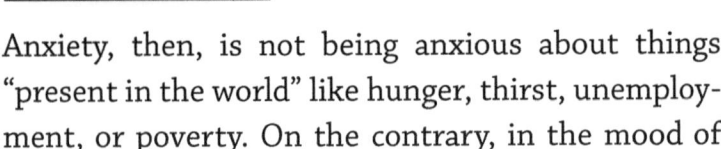

That in the face of which anxiety is anxious is nothing ready-to-hand within-the-world. But this "nothing ready-to-hand" [...] is not totally nothing.[24]

Anxiety, then, is not being anxious about things "present in the world" like hunger, thirst, unemployment, or poverty. On the contrary, in the mood of anxiety all that is "in the world" fades into the background. Also that routine orientation to the doings of "those around us", and thereby the dictatorship of the "they", seems to fade and no longer to offer any real support. This is why, when one is anxious, it doesn't help to be told: "Pull yourself together" or "Cheer up; no one is hurting you". Whatever people say, we feel exposed and unprotected. In the uncanny mood of anxiety *Dasein* is individualized or, as Heidegger says, "thrown back on itself", on its naked, pure "potentiality-for-being":

> [...] In anxiety there lies the possibility of a disclosure that is quite distinctive; for anxiety individualizes [...]. In this, Dasein is taken all the way back to its naked uncanniness, and becomes fascinated by it.[25]

What does Heidegger mean by this "possibility of a distinctive disclosure" through "individualization" and "naked uncanniness"? And what is it that *Dasein* is anxious about, if it is nothing concretely "in the world"? Heidegger's answer is baffling at first sight. *Dasein* is anxious about "nothing", but this "nothing" is "being-in-the-world" itself:

> If the "nothing" – that is, the world as such – exhibits itself as that in the face of which one has anxiety, this means that *being-in-the-world itself is that in the face of which anxiety is anxious.*[26]

Dasein, then, is anxious about its own "being-in-the-world", i.e. it is anxious about continuing to be "disclosingly" in this world and having to form and plan its own life. Anxiety here is a kind of "dread of life". Suddenly, the many individual cares and worries which had previously concerned us play no role any more. It is now the "care" character of *Dasein* per se that becomes a threat. We are anxious now not about anything concrete but about the very fact that "being-in-the-world" is a "caring" being, i.e. about our not being able to master the basic task of living.

Where the mood of anxiety really does bring a "fading" of the voices of the "they", including religious commandments about the sanctity of life, we notice that there is really nothing obliging us to go on living at all. Heidegger thus speaks of an anxiety in the face of "nothing", since "nothing" proves to be the basis of our existence:

The "nothing" with which anxiety brings us face to face unveils the nullity by which Dasein, in its very *basis*, is defined.[27]

But we must confront this "nullity" because it discloses for us the possibility of grounding ourselves in it and of authentic self-choice and self-creation. Despite its menacing aspect, then, "nothing" also signifies a "potentiality for being oneself":

> In uncanniness Dasein stands together with itself primordially. Uncanniness brings this entity face to face with its undisguised nullity, which belongs to the possibility of its ownmost potentiality-for-being.[28]

Anxiety reveals, then – just because it brings us face to face with "nothing" and thereby with the fact that nothing determines us – our potential freedom to choose our own self:

> Anxiety makes manifest in Dasein its *being towards* its ownmost potential for being – that is, its *being-free* for the freedom of choosing itself and taking hold of itself.[29]

But this "freedom of choosing oneself and taking hold of oneself" also includes the freedom not to choose oneself. In such a case one can either retreat from the mood of anxiety back into the seeming safety of the anonymous "they", or seize that most extreme possibility offered by existential freedom which is the radical refusal to accept "being-in-the-world" at all: i.e. suicide. But even as regards this menacing possibility of choosing death, Heidegger recommends an "anticipation of nothingness":

> Anticipation discloses to existence that its uttermost possibility lies in giving itself up, and thus it shatters all one's tenaciousness to whatever existence one has reached.[30]

Whereas for Christianity this "giving itself up" of a human existence is taboo (suicide being a sin and an offence to God), for Heidegger it is indeed an "uttermost possibility" of freedom. But – and here Heidegger's analysis of *Dasein* takes an interesting turn

– Man is not left to rely on himself alone in making his decision for or against life, for or against seizing a potential "being-oneself". We are, Heidegger says, just when confronted by this menacing "nothing" that puts our existence in question, called back into "being" by a mysterious voice: the "call of conscience".

The Call of Conscience

By "conscience" and "call of conscience" Heidegger does not at all mean what we normally associate with these words. He is not thinking of any moral or ethical scruples or "pangs of conscience", such as that which tells us "suicide is a sin", nor of any agency of self-control or self-critique that can be described by psychology. Neither is Heidegger's "conscience" the "super-ego" of Freud.

The "call of conscience" must rather be understood in an existential sense as a phenomenon of *Dasein*. It cannot be interpreted either as the voice of God or of any other metaphysical agency. But if it does not come from God or from a "super-ego" that can be

Heidegger's Central Idea

described in psychological terms, where does it come from? Who is it that calls and what is the call's content? Heidegger's answer is astounding:

> *What* does the conscience call to him to whom it appeals? Taken strictly, nothing. The call asserts nothing, gives no information about world events, has nothing to tell.

> Least of all does it try to set going a soliloquy in the self to which it has appealed. "Nothing" gets called to this self, but it has been *summoned* to itself – that is, to its own inmost potentiality-for-being.[31]

Nothing concrete, then – no "do this!" or "do that!" – is called out to *Dasein*. Rather, it is summoned to accept its own inmost potentiality for being-its-own-self. Who "summons" *Dasein* to do this? Is it perhaps God after all? Heidegger says "no" and offers a surprising but logically consistent alternative answer. The summoner is *Dasein* itself. Since for *Dasein*, due to its essential structure of "care", its own being is always a fundamental issue, *Dasein* itself makes itself heard in the uncanny mood of anxiety and calls itself, when faced with its own nothingness, back into being:

> To the extent that for *Dasein*, as care, its being is an issue, it [...] summons itself from its uncanniness towards its potentiality-for-being. The appeal calls back by calling forth [...] to the possibility of Dasein's taking over, in existing, even that thrown entity which it is.[32]

It is a matter, then, of taking over again one's own "thrown-ness" and thereby the basic existential structure of having to "pro-ject" one's own self. Or to put it more simply: it is a matter of accepting life's nature as a "task" and of committing oneself to this. Heidegger says that life itself tends to embolden us to take over the task of life. Thus, the human being is both "summoned" and "summoner" at once. As Heidegger puts it:

"The call comes *from* me and yet *from beyond* me."[33]

That our *Dasein* itself summons itself to take responsibility is a result of the existential structure of "care" as the basic character of human "being-in-the-world":

"Conscience *manifests itself* as the call *of care*. The caller is Dasein, which [...] is anxious about its potentiality-for-being."[34]

But it is also important, says Heidegger, that we follow this call and not close our "mind's ear" to it. We must be ready to hear it and to understand the summons as an opportunity:

> Hearing the appeal correctly is thus tantamount to having an understanding of oneself in one's ownmost potentiality-for-being – that is, to pro-jecting oneself upon one's *ownmost* authentic potentiality for becoming guilty.[35]

Heidegger means by this that it is only by deciding, in the face of "nothingness", that we want to live that we really take responsibility for our lives and our decisions. Every human existence is able, in principle, to do this. No one should, or even can, offer the excuse that he has not heard, or has not understood, the call, because:

> In understanding the call, Dasein is in thrall to its *ownmost possibility of existence*.[36]

Whether one hears this call "rightly" or not decides whether one is going to live one's life resolutely and responsibly or linger in the inauthenticity of conformity with the anonymous "they". Each of us has the chance to "choose his own self" here:

In so choosing, Dasein makes possible its ownmost "being-guilty", which remains closed off from the "they-self".[37]

Authentic and Inauthentic Existence

This is the sense, then, in which we can say that *Dasein* – the "being there" of a human being – is distinct from the "being there" of a stone. A stone, we might say, "is *there*" but a human being "*is* there". A human life does not live itself; it must be lived. It is we who decide just how we live it, just how we form it, just how our "being there" will be. But we can opt here either for authenticity or inauthenticity. Heidegger speaks of *Dasein* as a potentiality-for-being because it relates to its own being as a possibility for itself. *Dasein* thus appears before itself or, as Heidegger puts it, is "disclosed to itself":

Dasein *is* its disclosedness.[38]

This holds true, as we have shown, even when we let others dictate to us how we are to live, i.e. remain under the sway of the "they". Even here *Dasein* "disclos-

Heidegger's Central Idea

es" its existence to itself – but as an existence marked out for it by others.

For example, it might happen that a man grows up in a strictly religious family of the Amish type which rejects all industrial technology and uses oxen to plough the fields. Even if such a man remains attached, on into adulthood, to such a community and to its rules while really wanting to study engineering and travel abroad, his can still be said to be a *Dasein* which has, in its own way, "disclosed (its) world". It is just that, in this case, the *Dasein* "disclosed" is not a self-directed *Dasein* but one that – due to fear, laziness or weakness – exists as "they" expect it to. The man has chosen that one among several possibilities that is an inauthentic existence:

> Dasein always understands itself in terms of its existence – in terms of a possibility of itself: to be itself or not itself. Dasein has either chosen these possibilities itself, or got itself into them, or grown up in them already. Only the particular Dasein decides its existence, whether it does so by taking hold or by neglecting.[39]

Man thus spends his whole life in a condition defined by this choice: to resolutely take upon himself his own existence and "choose himself", or not. This is so because human life itself has, for Heidegger, this quality of "possibility":

> And because Dasein is in each case essentially its own possibility, it can, in its very being, "choose" itself and win itself [...]. But only in so far as it is essentially something which can be *authentic* – that is, something of its own – can it have lost itself and not yet won itself. As modes of being, *authenticity and inauthenticity* [...] are both grounded in the fact that any Dasein whatsoever is characterized by "mine-ness".[40]

Authenticity and inauthenticity are "modes of being": that is, different possibilities that *Dasein* has of forming its own life. The odd term "mine-ness" here means simply that it is, in each case, my own decision whether and how I live my life. But however I decide, I make this life, through this choice, my own life. My life is thus essentially distinguished from the lives of others which have been made, by their choice, theirs. Due to this essential "mine-ness" of *Dasein* I can never truly know how others, already or in future, "disclose" their existences. But for my own I am fully responsible.

This results in what Heidegger calls "guilt": namely, the existential onus weighing on each individual to stand by what he has chosen. Being an "onus" in this sense, Heidegger's "guilt" has nothing to do with "sin". It is neither a guilt before God nor a guilt that *Dasein* incurs by sometimes infringing laws or moral conventions:

Dasein is essentially guilty – not just guilty on *some occasions* and *on other occasions* not.[41]

Becoming Guilty Vis-à-Vis One's Own Existence

In an existential sense, then, *Dasein* is permanently "guilty" because a human being must constantly make decisions, seizing certain chances for self-development and thereby rejecting others. For example, if one decides to study mathematics, one cannot decide to train for a career as an actor, pianist, footballer or politician at the same time. If we lived forever, this would not be a problem. We could run one by one through all the studies and professions that attracted us, meet and marry countless delightful lovers from every clime, live in the desert, by the sea and also in the mountains – because our decisions would not, then, have to be rejections of other possibilities. If we were immortal, we could get around to everything sooner or later.

Were that the case, pure arbitrariness would replace existential decisions. But actual human life is radically different. Since our being, as Heidegger soberly states, is a "being-toward-death", each moment of our lives has its own unique value. Many chances only come once in a lifetime – and if we decide to let them pass, we cannot do later what we leave undone.

This is why Heidegger can say that we are "always already" guilty. Because regardless of whether we have made a good or a bad life-decision, the onus is always on us to stand by it:

> "*Being-guilty*" belongs to the being of Dasein itself and we have determined that this is primarily a "potentiality-for-being". Dasein "is" constantly guilty [...].⁴²

Dasein, then, is existentially guilty not vis-à-vis God, the law, or some received morality but vis-à-vis itself and its "potentiality-for-being". We are responsible for our life and also for the life we have not lived: for all the possibilities we did not seize and thereby withheld from our *Dasein*. Man must resolutely accept this kind of guilt by disclosing, through an existential "anticipation of death", the horizon of his own possibilities and his "potentiality-for-being" in its entirety and by acting in accordance with what is disclosed. The call of conscience helps us here by urging us to this choice and acceptance:

> The call is the call of care [...]. Hearing the appeal correctly is thus tantamount to having an understanding of oneself in one's *ownmost* potentiality-for-being –

> that is, to pro-jecting oneself upon one's ownmost authentic potentiality for becoming guilty [...]. In so choosing, Dasein makes possible its ownmost "being-guilty", which remains closed off from the "they-self".[43]

The inauthentic mode of being is distinct from the authentic one, then, in that the man who stays under the sway of the anonymous "they" allows others to make his decisions for him, or at least takes others' behaviour as his guide. But, considered existentially, he is still responsible for his decisions even when he does this and leaves unrealized his own potentiality for "being-guilty". Because even choosing not to choose is a choice.

The man, however, who accepts, out of the disclosedness of his "being-toward-death", his potentiality for being himself becomes, says Heidegger, able also to accept an "ownmost being-guilty". He stands by his own decisions in the face of his mortality and thereby gives to life as he lives it a denser and more intensive quality:

In understanding the call, Dasein lets its ownmost self *take action in itself* in terms of that potentiality-for-being which it has chosen.[44]

The humain aim that becomes visible through the structural analysis of *Dasein* must be: each human being's breaking free of the seductive comfort of the anonymous "they" and disclosing their own being in the authenticity of its "mine-ness".

This is not a normative, idealistic or moral idea; nor is it any divine or metaphysical aim. Heidegger strongly emphasizes that it is simply a conclusion we must draw from the structure of *Dasein* itself:

> [...] Anticipatory resoluteness (does not) stem from "idealistic" exactions soaring above existence and its possibilities. It springs from a sober understanding of what are, factically, the basic possibilities for Dasein.[45]

Man thus always has, in principle, the chance to resolutely form, in accordance with the "care" character of existence, his own life. Since Man's whole life is inevitably played out within the horizon of time, part of this is the acceptance of being mortal.

This result that Heidegger arrives at in his book *Being and Time* does not, of course, yet answer the question of "the meaning of being". He wanted, therefore, to probe this question further in a planned second part. But this was never written. Still, *Being and Time* does partially phenomenologically decipher the "meaning of being" question, at least insofar as this arises out of the existential structure of individual human *Dasein*.

There were worked out here such *existentialia* as "being-in-the-world", "state of mind", "care", "disclosedness", "being-toward-death", and the potential for "authenticity" and "inauthenticity" vis-à-vis "anxiety" aroused by "nothingness". The meaning of human life thus consists, in the end, in leading, within the horizon of time and in the face of finitude and mortality, an authentic, self-chosen life.

But this was not all. Heidegger also dealt, in many lessons, essays and lectures, with social and historical developments, since these too form part of "being", understood as the world in its entirety.

Historical epochs each disclose, Heidegger argues, their respective "destining of being". This does not mean that individuals are not responsible for their own lives but it does mean that mankind has perceived the world very differently in each historical period. Just as the individual can fall under the sway of "inauthenticity", so can whole nations and societies develop a false, or at least blinkered, worldview. Today, argues Heidegger, we are in danger of being overrun by a purely technological perception of reality and of losing our openness to the meaning of being.

Man in the "Enframing" of Technology, and the "Turning"

Normally, we mean by technology all those mechanical, electronic and other aids which mankind has developed to make life easier. Such aids include tools, like hammers, drills and computers, or technical procedures, like that of smelting iron in blast furnaces. Such things have always served, says Heidegger, the purpose of furthering Man's ends:

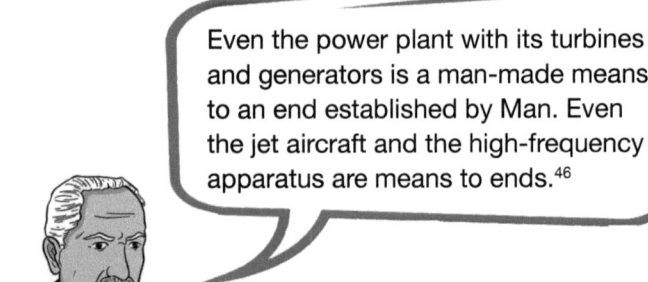

> Even the power plant with its turbines and generators is a man-made means to an end established by Man. Even the jet aircraft and the high-frequency apparatus are means to ends.[46]

But today, two hundred years after the start of the Industrial Revolution, technology is much more than just a means to the end of mastering Nature. Technology has gained such breathtaking triumphs, says

Heidegger, that it has altered our whole perception of the world. We no longer see Nature, the world, or even ourselves in a way free of preconceptions. Rather, one concern now governs all our perception: the instrumental one of "feasibility". One single question preoccupies us: what can be made possible and how? By means of what processes and procedures can we produce still more successfully and efficiently?

Technology is therefore no mere means. Technology is a way of revealing.[47]

To describe this new way Man has of disclosing and perceiving the world Heidegger uses the German word *"stellen"* which evokes several different but related ideas at once. Two of these are: Man's "ordering" or "setting" of Nature, and his "setting upon" it. Through technology, we "set" Nature, as a signalman "sets the points" on a railway. That is to say, we give to everything and everyone a specific order and direction. But this "setting" or "ordering" also involves an element of hostile domination; as users of technology, we also "set upon" Nature as one "sets upon" an enemy, or as a hunter "sets upon" his prey:

> Agriculture is now the mechanized food industry. Air is now set upon to yield nitrogen, the earth to yield ore, ore to yield uranium, for example; uranium is then set upon to yield atomic energy, which can be released either for destruction or for peaceful use.[48]

There is a great danger here, says Heidegger, that Man's use of technology may also be a case of our "setting upon" ourselves. Drawing on a third German connotation of the term *stellen*, Heidegger speaks of technology as a *"Ge-stell"*: a "framing" or "enframing". The danger is that Man has been "framed" by his own technology. We have begun to perceive the whole world, including our fellow men, in functional terms alone:

"Enframing" means the gathering together of that "setting-upon" which "sets upon" Man, i.e. challenges him forth to reveal the real, in the mode of ordering, as "standing-reserve".[49]

This term "standing-reserve" is another special coinage of Heidegger's. It evokes the idea that, today, when we disclose the being of our world, we disclose it only in the sense of a "stock-taking", making everything an object of calculation. Nature, for example, is "enframed" by the scientist in his experiments, which pose set questions to Nature and thus receive only set answers. The authentic meaning of being remains hidden here because no question is asked about it. Heidegger speaks here also of the "forgetfulness of being". We no longer disclose life or its meaning except in terms of "feasibility"; blinded by routine, we forget all life's other aspects. This "forgetfulness of being", Heidegger claims, has by now seized all areas of human life. Technological-scientific thought has established itself as thought's only recognized form. Its core is calculation.

Calculating thought now dominates not only Man's relations with Nature but also Man's with Man, because "technology" now includes a whole range of "social technologies". All thinking, Heidegger says, follows a single motto, expressed by Leibniz in the words *nihil est sine ratione* ("nothing is without reason"). But to say that every idea, theory, thesis, and statement must be backed up with reasons is to say that such ideas etc. must be calculable:

> Nothing is without reason. The principle now says that every thing counts as existing when and only when it has been securely established as a calculable object for cognition.[50]

This principle that "nothing is without reason" thus governs the very essence of our age. Every schoolchild knows that he must give reasons for what he thinks, that everything must be calculable and accountable. Every research department knows that what matters is to work out and build still more efficient machines. This logic of feasibility has become a law unto itself:

> Modern technology intractably presses toward bringing its contrivances and products to an all-embracing, greatest-possible perfection. This perfection consists in the completeness of the calculably secure establishing of objects, in the completeness of reckoning with them [...].⁵¹

The danger, Heidegger believed, lay in how the triumphs of technology seduce us into thinking that everything that can be calculated also makes sense and should be put into practice. He viewed, for example, very critically the great enthusiasm felt in the 1950s for atomic power, which had been calculated to be "completely safe" and the key to a world without worries. In an essay from 1957 he observed that the general euphoria was such that the whole age was being named after this new technology. This showed, he felt, how far we have already been "set upon" by technology in our search for meaning and see everything only from the viewpoint of feasibility. Whereas eras had once borne such names as "Humanism" or "the Age of Enlightenment",

> Humanity now enters an age to which it has given the name 'the Atomic Age'. A book that just appeared and that figured on having a broad readership bears the title 'We Will Live Through Atoms'. The book is equipped with a blurb by the Nobel Prize winner Otto Hahn and a preface by the current Minister of Defence Franz Josef Strauss. At the close of the introduction the author of the work writes: 'The Atomic Age can become a prosperous, happy age full of hope, an age in which we live through atoms. It all depends on us!' [52]

In view of the dangers of this energy-source, Heidegger holds the enthusiasm of such men as Hahn and Strauss for the idea that "we will live through atoms" to be highly questionable. He adds, with biting irony:

Certainly, it all depends on us. It depends on us and a few other things, namely, whether we still reflect, or whether in general we still can and want to reflect.[53]

The thinking of the atomic physicist and the Defence Minister, he goes on, lacks such reflection. If we want to survive, Heidegger says, we must dare to engage in a form of thought that goes beyond the merely instrumental reason of "calculation" and once again embraces the whole:

If we still want to enter on a path of reflection, then above all we must come to terms with the distinction that holds before our eyes the difference between mere calculative thinking and reflective thinking.[54]

In order to attain to this new reflective thinking Man must cast off the "enframing", that is, the technological perception of the world. Heidegger calls this "the turning". Such a "turning", indeed, cannot be the work of Man alone. It too, like technology and scientific thinking, is a part of the "destining of being". Because the technological worldview which considers nothing but feasibility is not some "work of the devil" but rather just one of the many eras of human history whose hour has slowly come around. But it is Heidegger's hope that, where technology attains a total dominance and its attendant catastrophes ensue, precisely this will give rise to a new reflective thinking. To express the inner dynamic of this "turning", Heidegger cites the poet Hölderlin:

But where danger is, (there) grows the saving power also.[55]

By this he means that the technological worldview eventually reaches its limits and sets free another kind of thought. Heidegger has no doubt that this is possible. Art and poetry already exemplify non-technological forms of thought and ways of disclosing being. Artists open up a spiritual access to the world that has its place quite beyond all calculative perception, since the products of art – paintings or pieces of music – cannot be measured by their "usefulness". Still, they "disclose the being of the world" in their way:

The essential nature of art would, then, be this: the setting-itself-to-work of the truth of beings.[56]

Art then, for Heidegger, is "truth setting itself (in)to (a) work". What he means by truth is very simple. Like the Ancient Greek philosophers he defines truth as *aletheia*, or unconcealedness. It is essential to Man that he has the possibility of perceiving this unconcealedness in what Heidegger calls "the clearing of being". Because Man, as we have seen, is not just any existing entity but an entity which "ex-ists", i.e. for which its existence is an *issue*. Man is thus always "held outside of himself" *into* this unconcealedness and "clearing of being". Reflective thinking allows us to become open to our own relation to truth as unconcealedness, outside the "enframing" of technology.

Of What Use is Heidegger's Discovery for Us Today?

Openness to the Mystery in the Age of Technology

Of what use to us is Heidegger's warning about technology? Heidegger was not an enemy of technology or progress. He knew that the growing technical mastery of the world was not to be stopped. Man has experimented, tested and researched since the dawn of history. Curiosity and the need to understand and control are an essential part of human existence, as are the sciences these produce:

Sciences are ways of being in which Dasein comports itself towards entities [...].[57]

Thus, the natural sciences and their technological way of disclosing the world are also a "way of being" of

Man by which he understands and controls entities, i.e. Nature. Heidegger fully recognized technology's massive achievements and, when he calls for reflection and a "turning", he does not mean a returning to some pre-industrial state of society. The "turning" is only a turning-away from the "forgetfulness of being". There exists a danger that the technological worldview might block off every other access to reality. Heidegger urges on us here a stance of "openness to the mystery" and "releasement" which would enable us to allow and accept the merits of technology while not being overwhelmed by them. Through this openness and "releasement" we have a chance of disclosing the world and ourselves in a way that transcends the technological worldview:

> I call the comportment which enables us to keep open to the meaning hidden in technology: *openness to the mystery*. Releasement towards things and openness to the mystery belong together. They grant us the possibility of dwelling in the world in a totally different way.[58]

"Releasement" and "openness to the mystery" mean, says Heidegger, that we can "leave the world be", so that it can reveal itself as it is, and not only as we think it has to be. Only where we "leave things be" in this way do our eyes open to what is essential in life.

Above all, we must not derive our self-understanding from technology alone. One can, then, concretely interpret what Heidegger is saying as: we may indeed enjoy the use of our computers, Internet, TV and cellphones – but we must not let these things define our lives. Heidegger would have considered what we often see today – people sustaining their identity only through the "enframing" of a virtual presence and self-presentation on Facebook and other technology-based social media – as a catastrophe:

> We can affirm the unavoidable use of technical devices and also deny them the right to dominate us, and so to warp, confuse, and lay waste our nature [...].

> We let technical devices enter our daily life and at the same time leave them outside; that is, let them alone, as things which are nothing absolute but remain dependent upon something higher.[59]

Also the advantages of modern molecular medicine, says Heidegger, can and should be enjoyed – but care must be taken to ensure that genetic engineering does not mean humanity's enslavement. Already in the 1950s he warned of how the future might bring the design and selection of "human material" and of the danger that technology's "enframing" might lead to sick human beings' becoming mere "clinical material" in hi-tech hospitals.

Even while making use of technology we need once again to open up our senses. If no such "turning" of thought occurs we shall fall increasingly victim to the "forgetfulness of being". Philosophy too, says Heidegger, shares in this "forgetfulness of being" within technology's "frame". For centuries it has defined Man exclusively as the *animal rationale*, and this has had its consequences:

> Humans are the reckoning creatures [...]. As modern European thinking, this thinking brought the world into the contemporary era, the atomic age.[60]

If we do not carry out the "turning" and do not succeed in making ourselves, through a state of openness and "releasement", addressable once again by being, we shall at some point become so bewitched by calculative thinking that we shall eventually "think past" that which is worthy of thought. But what is "worthy of thought" is being itself: the world in its wholeness, or life itself, whose meaning lies hidden under the "frame" of technology:

> If this is the way it's going to be, may we give up what is worthy of thought in favour of the recklessness of purely calculative thinking and its immense achievements? [...]. That is the question. It is the world-question of thinking. Answering this question decides what will become of the earth and of human existence on this earth.[61]

This question is as crucial in our own 21st as in Heidegger's 20th Century. Will we succumb to the recklessness of a merely calculative thinking? Or will we succeed in opposing, to the arithmetic of feasibility, capital and profit, a new human self-understanding?

Humanity's growing environmental awareness and the idea of sustainability may represent the first steps in a "turning" away from the "forgetfulness of being". But our continued over-exploitation of resources and exposure to technological catastrophe mean that we remain at a crossroads, so that Heidegger's plea that we understand ourselves no longer as masters, but rather as custodians, of being is as topical today as ever.

Anxiety is Part of Life – Existence as Potentiality

Another achievement of Heidegger's that is not to be undervalued is his destigmatizing and rehabilitating of the notion of anxiety. Before Heidegger anxiety was looked upon as something feeble, sickly and "unmanly". But his inclusion of this state within the analytic of *Dasein* has made possible an enlightened and positive attitude to this state of mind.

Heidegger's work even inspired a whole school of psychotherapy. "Existential psychoanalysis" has taken up the philosophical insights expounded in *Being and Time* and put them into therapeutic practice.

Renowned psychiatrists, neurologists and psychoanalysts such as Medard Boss and Ludwig Binswanger treated their patients on the basis of Heidegger's existential structures of *Dasein*. They saw mental illness as arising from an inauthentic, not-truly-lived life and tried to show their patients how their being bound into the anonymous "they" had caused compulsions and bad choices, thus empowering them with a new openness to life.

They performed a kind of phenomenological stocktaking of each patient's "being-in-the-world", thoroughly illuminating his lived reality and state of mind. In this way they enabled him to give free rein to his own feelings (in particular his anxiety) and finally restored him, where the therapy succeeded, to authentic life. Still today this liberation from the restraints of the anonymous "they" and the giving of free rein to anxiety play a large role in many psychotherapeutic treatments.

We owe it to Heidegger that, in the 21st Century, we no longer look upon anxiety as a character flaw, weakness or deformity but rather as an essential part of what it is to be human indispensable to the individual's mastery of his own life:

Anxiety [...] springs from Dasein *itself*.[62]

Anxiety is a part of life. There is hardly anyone who has not found himself faced with the problem of feeling unable, in the short or long term, to perform his daily duties. Everyone knows what it is to be afraid of losing one's job, of being left by a spouse or partner, of loneliness, sickness, old age and death. Often such problems meld into an anxiety about existence that no longer has any concrete object. One has the feeling then of not being able to shoulder the task of life at all. But menacing though it may be, this uncanny anxiety about "being-in-the-world" has a positive side to it.

It is Heidegger's merit that he pointed this out. Menacing as the mood of anxiety is, since it confronts us with the radical possibility of "non-being", it has a liberating core. It discloses to us our "ownmost" freedom to resolutely confront nothingness:

Anxiety makes manifest in Dasein its *being towards* its ownmost potentiality-for-being – that is, *its being-free* for the freedom of choosing itself.[63]

Thus, anxiety opens up the character of possibility inherent in life as essentially a "being-free" to stand by one's own life:

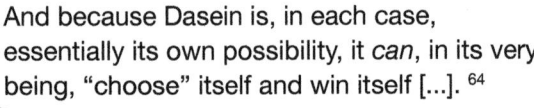

And because Dasein is, in each case, essentially its own possibility, it *can*, in its very being, "choose" itself and win itself [...]. [64]

Strange as it may sound, it is precisely the chapter on "anxiety" in *Being and Time* that can be most emboldening. Anyone who has ever been in such a state of mind – feeling abandoned, and suffering a subversive anxiety about dealing with his own life – will know that one can emerge stronger from an encounter with "rock bottom". The cares and fears of the past are suddenly put into perspective and one learns to appreciate what is really important. Anxiety can also be an indication that something is not right and that an entirely new path must be taken. In some such cases medical help may be required. But one thing is certain: anxiety, preeminent among the *existentialia*, is, as Heidegger shows us, a part of *Dasein*'s "care character" and thus a part of life.

Breaking Away from the Anonymous "They"

If we ask the question "what use is Heidegger's discovery for us today?" a part of the answer must certainly be: his call to "authenticity" remains as relevant as ever. Above all in today's societies, due to the ubiquity of market forces and the omnipresence of the media, we see ever greater and deeper-reaching compulsions to conform which seduce us into the "inauthentic" mode of being typical of the anonymous "they".

Since ever more people's jobs are temporary or insecure, the pressure to "adapt" is ever greater. Today, "one" is flexible, motivated, and willing to commute long distances or even move home to get or keep a job – and, thus, so must each concrete individual be too. "One" is what "one" earns and "one" earns what "one" is. University study too is increasingly focussed on the economic aim of improving "one"'s earning potential in the shortest possible time. In many countries education systems, starved of funds, are yielding up their charges to the anonymous "they" of a society geared to production alone. "One" has no time to lose; "one" must do one's internship abroad;

and "one" must enter the labour market as young and as narrowly-focussed as possible.

In social life too, we see millions of so-called "profiles" on Facebook and other social media presenting images that "one must" comply with if "one" is to be seen as interesting and attractive. And such mass entertainments as TV "talent shows" reinforce the sway of this anonymous "one" over the "I" by illustrating, on the most simple-minded level, "what one needs" to be a success.

Within these pre-set material production-imperatives of modern society there seems to be less and less place for authentic existence as a self-chosen, "ownmost" potential for being. If the anonymous "they" is not on the rise, then it certainly exerts a huge gravitational force. But Heidegger urges us to take the risk of authenticity and to hearken to the call of conscience which calls us back out of inauthentic self-loss. As we have seen, it is *Dasein* itself that calls us to take responsibility here:

> In understanding the call, Dasein is in thrall to *its ownmost possibility of existence*.[65]

Of What Use is Heidegger's Discovery for Us Today?

But is this really reasonable? Is it really the case that *Dasein* itself calls itself back into its authenticity? Is there really such an inner voice or is this all just a matter of fine words and sonorous formulations on Heidegger's part?

Adorno, a philosopher inspired by dialectical materialism, called Heidegger's philosophy a "jargon of authenticity". Heidegger hid, Adorno claimed, behind mere formal determinations and offered to the individual, in the end, no rationally comprehensible criteria for his decisions; it was for this reason that Heidegger produced an apolitical philosophy which focussed only on *existentialia* and had nothing to say of history, human rights, or the political struggle for liberation. No wonder then, Adorno concluded, that Heidegger was actively, or at the very least passively, complicit in the Nazi regime that ruled his homeland from 1933 to 1945.

It is indeed the case that Heidegger was forbidden to teach at German universities for six years after the war because he had been a member of the Nazi party. Still today his actions during the Hitler regime remain a subject of controversy.

We know for a fact that Heidegger did join the party in May 1933 just a few days after having been appointed, by the Nazi authorities, as rector of Freiburg University. He personally handed a notice of dismissal to his philosophical mentor and friend, the phenomenologist Professor Husserl who, as a Jew, could no longer teach in Nazi Germany. He even praised, in his inaugural address as rector, the German state under Hitler, as "the consummation of historical development" and held to this enthusiastic line even when one of his most brilliant students (and his lover) Hannah Arendt, had later that year, being a Jewess, to flee the country.

Only a whole year later, after the terrible "Night of the Long Knives" in which Hitler had a thousand members of his own party murdered by the SS, did Heidegger, as he later claimed, realize that Nazism was not aiming at an all-embracing, egalitarian community of the people but rather at a brutal technocratic biologism. It was only then that he stepped down as rector. Admittedly, from then on Heidegger found himself under close surveillance.

He also made such gestures of opposition as refusing to donate to the Nazi-run University League and can thus be said to have clearly rejected National Socialism after a year. But throughout all the rest of his life he never really addressed this grave, even if temporary, moral error. The question continued to hang over him of why he, a great philosopher, had not emigrated or resisted.

One of his students, Marcuse – like Adorno a thinker in the dialectical materialist tradition – once said that it was impossible to separate the man Heidegger from his philosophy. But the man's flaws seemed not to detract from the interest in his work.

Being and Time continued to be read all over the world and by the end of the 20th Century "Heidegger studies" were a veritable industry, with over 2000 books published in the field. Although debate continues about whether his life cast a shadow on his work – or whether indeed there is something politically inadequate or questionable in his analysis of *Dasein* itself – his influence particularly on French existentialism and structuralism was enormous.

His new perspective on Man; his drawing into philosophy of moods and states of mind; and his key idea of an existential opening-up of *Dasein* – these are surely of timeless significance. Heidegger made it unmistakably clear to us that the human individual always has the potential either to be himself or not be himself. This is the spur to human action that he revealed:

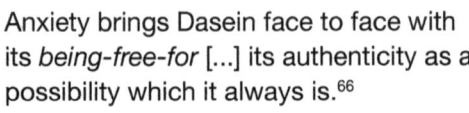

> Anxiety brings Dasein face to face with its *being-free-for* [...] its authenticity as a possibility which it always is.[66]

The call that goes out from *Dasein* calling *Dasein* itself back into its own authenticity is, in the end, no mere formal determination but is borne out by real psychological phenomena. Heidegger repeatedly points out that we can actually feel, in every second, our disclosedness-to-being and thus our being-in-the-world:

> *Mood* has already disclosed, in every case, *being-in-the-world as a whole*.[67]

Whoever lives an inauthentic life may not suffer constant unhappiness, but he will feel from time to time that something else or something more is possible for him and will not entirely accept his fate. But he who succeeds in recognizing his "ownmost" aspirations and in making of these his project for a self and a life will not be discouraged by obstacles or setbacks. Each of us knows immediately, through our "state of mind", how it stands with us in this respect:

In a "state of mind" Dasein is always brought before itself and has always found itself – not in the sense of coming across itself by perceiving itself but in the sense of finding itself in the mood that it has.[68]

Our state of mind, then, tells us whether we are living in a manner true to ourselves or whether we need to change.

Living with Mortality – Living with Resoluteness!

Heidegger urges us to make awareness of death a part of life. It is wrong to repress this awareness and to act as if we will live forever. He encourages us, indeed, to focus openly on the concrete reality of our own individual death. It is in the willed "anticipation" of our death that we achieve an experience of finitude that both renders anxious and gives support:

> Anticipation reveals to Dasein its lostness in the "they-self" and brings it face to face with the possibility of being itself [...] in an impassioned *freedom-towards-death*: a freedom which has been released from the illusions of the "they" and which is factical, certain of itself, and anxious.[69]

Is this attractive? Is it not rather a burdening and limiting of the quality of life? Which of us really wants to think, every day, of his own death and to make his decisions in this "anticipation" of mortality? Heidegger speaks in the passage cited of an "impassioned freedom-towards-death".

Just because the engagement with one's own mortality is stated here to be an "impassioned" one, Heidegger clearly does not mean that we should think of death every five minutes and be aware of our mortality, for example, when buying a new sofa. This would be both absurd and impossible. Nor is Heidegger urging us to "live every day as if it were our our last". This would also be a trivializing interpretation of what he calls "anticipation" and would miss the point of his analysis of *Dasein*.

Heidegger makes it clear from the start that all of us (himself included) for the most part "evade" the thought of death in our everyday lives:

> Our everyday falling evasion *in the face of death* is an *inauthentic being-towards-death* [...]. Inauthenticity characterizes a kind of being into which Dasein can divert itself and has for the most part always diverted itself; but Dasein does not necessarily and constantly have to divert itself into this kind of being.[70]

The point is, then, that *Dasein* should not constantly divert itself from the awareness of mortality. "Anticipation" must be there, but it is reserved for special moments, moods or phases of life. In his late work particularly, Heidegger points up that this experience of finitude which draws *Dasein* into an encounter with being as a whole can occur not only in and through the state of mind of anxiety but also in and through that of "releasement". As soon as we succeed in simply *letting be* all our little daily cares, our stress with our job, and our money-worries it proves possible to see life in a more all-embracing light. "Anticipation of death" is important as an existential experience to the extent that it helps us to resolutely form our lives and give them meaning:

> Only an entity which, in its being, is essentially *futural*, so that it is free for its death and can let itself be thrown back upon its factical "there" by shattering itself against death [...] can [...] take over its own thrownness and be *in the moment of vision* for "its time".[71]

Someone, for example, who denies his mortality completely and "projects" his life and self as those of an ageless, deathless being is surely "projecting" far too much and will suffer from failing, wholly or largely, to achieve his life-aims. He must then either take stock more soberly or live out to the bitter end a self-harried, restless life without satisfaction or inner peace.

Conversely, someone can "project" too unassuming a self and life and make too few demands on himself. One pays for this with the feeling that one has frittered away one's life. This is why it is important to "disclose" one's possibilities realistically through the anticipation of death.

Drawing our own mortality into life helps us to seek out and accept new challenges. Because it is only in the face of death that *Dasein* exists in full intensity and takes on responsibility for seizing or failing to seize opportunities for forming and shaping its life.

It is true that something heavy, brooding and sombre haunts Heidegger's analysis of *Dasein*. But despite his emphasis on the "uncanniness" of the mood of anxiety, Heidegger's main aim was always to disclose, in a positive way, *Dasein*'s character of "potentiality". When he speaks of "being-towards-death" and of "wanting-to-have-a-conscience" he is evoking, in the last analysis, a clearly affirmative attitude to life which culminates in resolute activity:

> [...] "Wanting-to-have-a-conscience", which has been made determinate as "being-towards-death" (does not) signify a kind of seclusion in which one flees the world. Rather it brings one, without illusions, into the resoluteness of "taking action".[72]

Bibliographical References:

1. Martin Heidegger, *Being and Time* (translated by John MacQuarrie and Edward Robinson) Blackwell Publishers, Oxford, 2001, p. 33.
2. Ibid. p. 27
3. Ibid. p. 32
4. Ibid. p. 76
5. Ibid. p. 23
6. Ibid. p. 58
7. Ibid. p. 89
8. Ibid. p. 173
9. Ibid. p. 236
10. Martin Heidegger, Phenomenological Interpretations with Respect to Aristotle: Indication of the Hermeneutical Situation, translated by Martin Baur, Man and World, 25 (1992) p. 361
11. Martin Heidegger, *Being and Time* (translated by John MacQuarrie and Edward Robinson) Blackwell Publishers, Oxford, 2001, p. 185
12. Ibid.
13. Ibid. pps. 185-86
14. Ibid. p. 303
15. Ibid. pps. 276-77
16. Ibid. p. 302
17. Ibid. p. 298
18. Ibid. p. 308
19. Ibid. p. 151
20. Ibid. p. 164
21. Ibid. p. 312
22. Ibid. p. 313
23. Ibid
24. Ibid. pps. 231-232
25. Ibid. p. 235 and p. 394
26. Ibid. p. 232
27. Ibid. p. 356
28. Ibid. p. 333
29. Ibid. p. 232
30. Ibid. p. 308

31 Ibid. p. 318
32 Ibid. p. 333
33 Ibid. p. 320
34 Ibid. p. 322
35 Ibid. p. 333-34
36 Ibid. p. 334
37 Ibid.
38 Ibid. p. 171
39 Ibid. p. 33
40 Ibid. p. 68
41 Ibid. p. 353
42 Ibid.
43 Ibid. pps. 333-34
44 Ibid. p. 334
45 Ibid. p. 358
46 Martin Heidegger, The Question Concerning Technology and Other Essays, translated by William Lovitt, Garland Publishing, New York and London, 1977, p. 5
47 Ibid. p. 12
48 Ibid. p. 15
49 Ibid. p. 20
50 Martin Heidegger On the Principle of Reason, translated by Reginald Lilly, Indiana University Press, 1991, p. 120
51 Ibid. p. 121
52 Ibid. pps. 121-22
53 Ibid. p. 122
54 Ibid.
55 Martin Heidegger, The Question Concerning Technology and Other Essays, translated by William Lovitt, Garland Publishing, New York and London, 1977, p. 28
56 The Origin of the Work of Art, in Martin Heidegger, Off the Beaten Track, edited and translated by Julian Young and Kenneth Haynes, Cambridge University Press, 2002, p. 16
57 Martin Heidegger, *Being and Time* (translated by John MacQuarrie and Edward Robinson) Blackwell Publishers, Oxford, 2001, p. 33
58 Martin Heidegger, Discourse on Thinking, translated by John M. Anderson and E. Hans Freund, Harper Torchbooks, New York, p.55

59 Ibid. p. 54
60 Martin Heidegger On the Principle of Reason,
    translated by Reginald Lilly, Indiana University Press, 1991, p. 129.
61 Ibid.
62 Martin Heidegger, *Being and Time* (translated by John MacQuarrie
    and Edward Robinson) Blackwell Publishers, Oxford, 2001, p. 395
63 Ibid. p. 232
64 Ibid. p. 68
65 Ibid. p. 334
66 Ibid. p. 232
67 Ibid. p. 176
68 Ibid. p. 174
69 Ibid. p. 311
70 Ibid. p. 303
71 Ibid. p. 437
72 Ibid. pps. 357-58

Already published in the same series:

Walther Ziegler
Camus in 60 Minutes
ISBN 9783741227738

Walther Ziegler
Freud in 60 Minutes
ISBN 9783741227707

Walther Ziegler
Hegel in 60 Minutes
ISBN 9783741227677

Walther Ziegler
Heidegger in 60 Minutes
ISBN 9783741227752

Walther Ziegler
Kant in 60 Minutes
ISBN 9783741226373

Walther Ziegler
Marx in 60 Minutes
ISBN 9783741227691

Walther Ziegler
Platon in 60 Minutes
ISBN 9783741227615

Walther Ziegler
Rousseau in 60 Minutes
ISBN 9783741227622

Walther Ziegler
Sartre in 60 Minutes
ISBN 9783741227653

Walther Ziegler
Smith in 60 Minutes
ISBN 9783741227721

Coming soon in the same series:

Walther Ziegler
Adorno in 60 Minutes

Walther Ziegler
Arendt in 60 Minutes

Walther Ziegler
Bacon in 60 Minutes

Walther Ziegler
Descartes in 60 Minutes

Walther Ziegler
Foucault in 60 Minutes

Walther Ziegler
Habermas in 60 Minutes

Walther Ziegler
Hobbes in 60 Minutes

Walther Ziegler
Nietzsche in 60 Minutes

Walther Ziegler
Popper in 60 Minutes

Walther Ziegler
Rawls in 60 Minutes

Walther Ziegler
Schopenhauer in 60 Minutes

Walther Ziegler
Wittgenstein in 60 Minutes

The author:

Dr Walther Ziegler is academically trained in the fields of philosophy, history and political science. As a foreign correspondent, reporter and newsroom coordinator for the German TV station ProSieben he has produced films on every continent. His news reports have won several prizes and awards. He has also authored numerous books in the field of philosophy. His many years of experience as a journalist mean that he is able to present the complex ideas of the great philosophers in a way that is both engaging and very clear. Since 2007 he has also been active as a teacher and trainer of young TV journalists in Munich, holding the post of Academic Director at the Media Academy, an institute of higher education that offers film and TV courses at its base directly on the site of the major European film production company Bavaria Film.